# Ethics of Kautilya

Ratan Lal Basu

Published by Kautilya, 2024.

While every precaution has been taken in the preparation of this book, the publisher assumes no responsibility for errors or omissions, or for damages resulting from the use of the information contained herein.

ETHICS OF KAUTILYA

**First edition. July 31, 2024.**



ISBN: 979-8227826787

Written by Ratan Lal Basu.

# Ethics of Kautilya
# Ratan Lal Basu

Contents

# Chapter 1: Chanakya Niti

Section-1

1. Humbly bowing down before the almighty Lord Sri Vishnu, the Lord of the three worlds, I recite maxims of the science of political ethics (niti) selected from the various satras.

2. That man who by the study of these maxims from the satras acquires a knowledge of the most celebrated principles of duty, and understands what ought and what ought not to be followed, and what is good and what is bad, is most excellent.

3. Therefore with an eye to the public good, I shall speak that which, when understood, will lead to an understanding of things in their proper perspective.

4. Even a pandit comes to grief by giving instruction to a foolish disciple, by maintaining a wicked wife, and by excessive familiarity with the miserable.

5. A wicked wife, a false friend, a saucy servant and living in a house with a serpent in it are nothing but death.

6. One should save his money against hard times, save his wife at the sacrifice of his riches, but invariably one should save his soul even at the sacrifice of his wife and riches.

7. Save your wealth against future calamity. Do not say, "What fear has a rich man of calamity?" When riches begin to forsake one even the accumulated stock dwindles away.

8. Do not inhabit a country where you are not respected, cannot earn your livelihood, have no friends, or cannot acquire knowledge.

9. Do not stay for a single day where there are not these five persons: a wealthy man, a Brahmana well versed in Vedic lore, a king, a river and a physician.

10. Wise men should never go into a country where there are no means of earning one's livelihood, where the people have no dread of

anybody, have no sense of shame, no intelligence, or a charitable disposition.

11. Test a servant while in the discharge of his duty, a relative in difficulty, a friend in adversity, and a wife in misfortune.

12. He is a true friend who does not forsake us in time of need, misfortune, famine, or war, in a king's court, or at the crematorium (smashana).

13. He who gives up what is imperishable for that which is perishable, loses that which is imperishable; and doubtlessly loses that which is perishable also.

14. A wise man should marry a virgin of a respectable family even if she is deformed. He should not marry one of a low-class family, though beautiful. Marriage in a family of equal status is preferable.

15. Do not put your trust in rivers, men who carry weapons, beasts with claws or horns, women, and members of a royal family.

16. Even from poison extract nectar, wash and take back gold if it has fallen in filth, receive the highest knowledge (Krishna consciousness) from a low born person; so also a girl possessing virtuous qualities (stri-ratna) even if she be born in a disreputable family.

17. Women have hunger two-fold, shyness four-fold, daring six-fold, and lust eight-fold as compared to men.

18. Untruthfulness, rashness, guile, stupidity, avarice, uncleanliness and cruelty are a women's seven natural f laws.

19. To have ability for eating when dishes are ready at hand, to be robust and virile in the company of one's religiously wedded wife, and to have a mind for making charity when one is prosperous are the fruits of no ordinary austerities.

20. He whose son is obedient to him, whose wife's conduct is in accordance with his wishes, and who is content with his riches, has his heaven here on earth.

21. They alone are sons who are devoted to their father. He is a father who supports his sons. He is a friend in whom we can confide, and

she only is a wife in whose company the husband feels contented and peaceful.

22. Avoid him who talks sweetly before you but tries to ruin you behind your back, for he is like a pitcher of poison with milk on top.

23. Do not put your trust in a bad companion nor even trust an ordinary friend, for if he should get angry with you, he may bring all your secrets to light.

24. Do not reveal what you have thought upon doing, but by wise council keep it secret being determined to carry it into execution.

25. Foolishness is indeed painful, and verily so is youth, but more painful by far than either is being obliged in another person's house.

26. There does not exist a ruby in every mountain, nor a pearl in the head of every elephant; neither are the sadhus to be found everywhere, nor sandal trees in every forest.

27. Wise men should always bring up their sons in various moral ways, for children who have knowledge of niti-sastra and are well-behaved become a glory to their family.

28. Those parents who do not educate their sons are their enemies; for as is a crane among swans, so are ignorant so are ignorant sons in a public assembly.

29. Many a bad habit is developed through overindulgence, and many a good one by chastisement, therefore beat your son as well as your pupil; never indulge them. ("Spare the rod and spoil the child.")

30. Let not a single day pass without your learning a verse, half a verse, or a fourth of it, or even one letter of it; nor without attending to charity, study and other pious activity.

31. Separation from the wife, disgrace from one's own people, an enemy saved in battle, service to a wicked king, poverty, and a mismanaged assembly: these six kinds of evils, if afflicting a person, burn him even without fire.

32. Trees on a river bank, a woman in another man's house, and kings without counsellors go without doubt to swift destruction.

33. A Brahmana's strength is in his learning, a king's strength is in his army, a vaishya's strength is in his wealth and a shudra's strength is in his attitude of service.

34. The prostitute has to forsake a man who has no money, the subject a king that cannot defend him, the birds a tree that bears no fruit, and the guests a house after they have finished their meals.

34. Brahmanas quit their patrons after receiving alms from them, scholars leave their teachers after receiving education from them, and animals desert a forest that has been burnt down.

36. He who befriends a man whose conduct is vicious, whose vision impure, and who is notoriously crooked, is rapidly ruined.

37. Friendship between equals flourishes, service under a king is respectable, it is good to be business-minded in public dealings, and a handsome lady is safe in her own home.

38. In this world, whose family is there without blemish? Who is free from sickness and grief? Who is forever happy?

39. A man's descent may be discerned by his conduct, his country by his pronunciation of language, his friendship by his warmth and glow, and his capacity to eat by his body.

40. Give your daughter in marriage to a good family, engage your son in learning, see that your enemy comes to grief, and engage your friends in dharma. (Krsna consciousness).

41. Of a rascal and a serpent, the serpent is the better of the two, for he strikes only at the time he is destined to kill, while the former at every step.

42. Therefore kings gather round themselves men of good families, for they never forsake them either at the beginning, the middle or the end.

43. At the time of the pralaya (universal destruction) the oceans are to exceed their limits and seek to change, but a saintly man never changes.

44. Do not keep company with a fool for as we can see he is a two-legged beast. Like an unseen thorn he pierces the heart with his sharp words.

45. Though men be endowed with beauty and youth and born in noble families, yet without education they are like the palasa flower which is void of sweet fragrance.

46. The beauty of a cuckoo is in its notes, that of a woman in her unalloyed devotion to her husband, that of an ugly person in his scholarship, and that of an ascetic in his forgiveness.

47. Give up a member to save a family, a family to save a village, a village to save a country, and the country to save yourself.

48. There is no poverty for the industrious. Sin does not attach itself to the person practicing japa (chanting of the holy names of the Lord). Those who are absorbed in maunam (silent contemplation of the Lord) have no quarrel with others. They are fearless who remain always alert.

49. What is too heavy for the strong and what place is too distant for those who put forth effort? What country is foreign to a man of true learning? Who can be inimical to one who speaks pleasingly?

50. As a whole forest becomes fragrant by the existence of a single tree with sweet-smelling blossoms in it, so a family becomes famous by the birth of a virtuous son.

51. As a single withered tree, if set aflame, causes a 3whole forest to burn, so does a rascal son destroy a whole family.

52. As night looks delightful when the moon shines, so is a family gladdened by even one learned and virtuous son.

53. What is the use of having many sons if they cause grief and vexation? It is better to have only one son from whom the whole family can derive support and peacefulness.

54. Fondle a son until he is five years of age, and use the stick for another ten years, but when he has attained his sixteenth year treat him as a friend.

55. He who runs away from a fearful calamity, a foreign invasion, a terrible famine, and the companionship of wicked men is safe.

56 He who has not acquired one of the following: religious merit (dharma), wealth (artha), satisfaction of desires (Kama), or liberation (moksa) is repeatedly born to die.

57. Lakshmi, the Goddess of wealth, comes of Her own accord where fools are not respected, grain is well stored up, and the husband and wife do not quarrel.

58. These five: the life-span, the type of work, wealth, learning and the time of one's death are determined while one is in the womb.

59. Offspring, friends and relatives flee from a devotee of the Lord: yet those who follow him bring merit to their families through their devotion.

60. Fish, tortoises, and birds bring up their young by means of sight, attention and touch; so do saintly men afford protection to their associates by the same means.

61. As long as your body is healthy and under control and death is distant, try to save your soul; when death is immanent what can you do?

62. Learning is like a cow of desire. It, like her, yields in all seasons. Like a mother, it feeds you on your journey. Therefore learning is a hidden treasure.

63. A single son endowed with good qualities is far better than a hundred devoid of them. For the moon, though one, dispels the darkness, which the stars, though numerous, cannot.

64. A still-born son is superior to a foolish son endowed with a long life. The first causes grief for but a moment while the latter like a blazing fire consumes his parents in grief for life.

65. Residing in a small village devoid of proper living facilities, serving a person born of a low family, unwholesome food, a frowning wife, a foolish son, and a widowed daughter burn the body without fire.

66. What good is a cow that neither gives milk nor conceives? Similarly, what is the value of the birth of a son if he becomes neither learned nor a pure devotee of the Lord?

67. When one is consumed by the sorrows of life, three things give him relief: offspring, a wife, and the company of the Lord's devotees.

68. Kings speak for once, men of learning once, and the daughter is given in marriage once. All these things happen once and only once.

69. Religious austerities should be practiced alone, study by two, and singing by three. A journey should be undertaken by four, agriculture by five, and war by many together.

70. She is a true wife who is clean (suci), expert, chaste, pleasing to the husband, and truthful. 71. The house of a childless person is a void, all directions are void to one who has no relatives, the heart of a fool is also void, but to a poverty stricken man all is void.

72. Scriptural lessons not put into practice are poison; a meal is poison to him who suffers from indigestion; a social gathering is poison to a poverty stricken person; and a young wife is poison to an aged man.

73. That man who is without religion and mercy should be rejected. A guru without spiritual knowledge should be rejected. The wife with an offensive face should be given up, and so should relatives who are without affection.

74. Constant travel brings old age upon a man; a horse becomes old by being constantly tied up; lack of sexual contact with her husband brings old age upon a woman; and garments become old through being left in the sun.

75. Consider again and again the following: the right time, the right friends, the right place, the right means of income, the right ways of spending, and from whom you derive your power.

76. For the twice-born the fire (Agni) is a representative of God. The Supreme Lord resides in the heart of His devotees. Those of average intelligence (alpa-buddhi or kanista-adhikari) see God only in His

sri-murti (deity form), but those of broad vision see the Supreme Lord everywhere.

77. Agni is the worshipable person for the twice-born; the Brahmana for the other castes; the husband for the wife; and the guest who comes for food at the midday meal for all.

78. As gold is tested in four ways by rubbing, cutting, heating and beating— so a man should be tested by these four things: his renunciation, his conduct, his qualities and his actions.

79. A thing may be dreaded as long as it has not over4taken you, but once it has come upon you, try to get rid of it without hesitation.

80. Though persons be born from the same womb and under the same stars, they do not become alike in disposition as the thousand fruits of the badari tree.

81. He whose hands are clean does not like to hold an office; he who desires nothing cares not for bodily decorations; he who is only partially educated cannot speak agreeably; and he who speaks out plainly cannot be a deceiver.

82. The learned are envied by the foolish; rich men by the poor; chaste women by adulteresses; and beautiful ladies by ugly ones.

83. Indolent application ruins study; money is lost when entrusted to others; a farmer who sows his seed sparsely is ruined; and an army is lost for want of a commander.

84. Learning is retained through putting into practice; family prestige is maintained through good behaviour; a respectable person is recognised by his excellent qualities; and anger is seen in the eyes.

85. Religion is preserved by wealth; knowledge by diligent practice; a king by conciliatory words; and a home by a dutiful housewife.

86. Those who blaspheme Vedic wisdom, who ridicule the life style recommended in the satras, and who deride men of peaceful temperament, come to grief unnecessarily.

87. Charity puts an end to poverty; righteous conduct to misery; discretion to ignorance; and scrutiny to fear.

88. There is no disease (so destructive) as lust; no enemy like infatuation; no fire like wrath; and no happiness like spiritual knowledge.

89. A man is born alone and dies alone; and he experiences the good and bad consequences of his karma alone; and he goes alone to hell or the Supreme abode.

90. Heaven is but a straw to him who knows spiritual life; so is life to a valiant man; a woman to him who has subdued his senses; and the universe to him who is without attachment for the world.

91. Learning is a friend on the journey; a wife in the house; medicine in sickness; and religious merit is the only friend after death.

92. Rain which falls upon the sea is useless; so is food for one who is satiated; in vain is a gift for one who is wealthy; and a burning lamp during the daytime is useless.

93. There is no water like rainwater; no strength like one's own; no light like that of the eyes; and no wealth dearer than food grain.

94. The poor wish for wealth; animals for the faculty of speech; men wish for heaven; and godly persons for liberation.

95. The earth is supported by the power of truth; it is the power of truth that makes the sun shine and the winds blow; indeed all things rest upon truth.

96. The Goddess of wealth is unsteady (chanchala), and so is the life breath. The duration of life is uncertain, and the place of habitation is uncertain; but in all this inconsistent world religious merit alone is immovable.

97. Among men the barber is cunning; among birds the crow; among beasts the jackal; and among women, the malin (flower girl).

98. These five are your fathers; he who gave you birth, girdled you with sacred thread, teaches you, provides you with food, and protects you from fearful situations.

99. These five should be considered as mothers; the king's wife, the preceptor's wife, the friend's wife, your wife's mother, and your own mother.

100. By means of hearing one understands dharma, malignity vanishes, knowledge is acquired, and liberation from material bondage is gained.

101. Among birds the crow is vile; among beasts the dog; the ascetic whose sins is abominable, but he who blasphemes others is the worst chandala.

102. Brass is polished by ashes; copper is cleaned by tamarind; a woman, by her menses; and a river by its f low.

103. The king, the Brahmana, and the ascetic yogi who go abroad are respected; but the woman who wanders is utterly ruined.

104. He who has wealth has friends. He who is wealthy has relatives. The rich one alone is called a man, and the affluent alone are respected as pandits.

105. As is the desire of Providence, so functions one's intellect; one's activities are also controlled by Providence; and by the will of Providence one is surrounded by helpers.

106. Time perfects all living beings as well as kills them; it alone is awake when all others are asleep. Time is insurmountable.

107. Those born blind cannot see; similarly blind are those in the grip of lust. Proud men have no perception of evil; and those bent on acquiring riches see no sin in their actions.

108. The spirit soul goes through his own course of karma and he himself suffers the good and bad results thereby accrued. By his own actions he entangles himself in samsara, and by his own efforts he extricates himself.

109. The king is obliged to accept the sins of his subjects; the purohit (priest) suffers for those of the king; a husband suffers for those of his wife; and the guru suffers for those of his pupils.

Section-2

110. A father who is a chronic debtor, an adulterous mother, a beautiful wife, and an unlearned son are enemies ( in one's own home).

111. Conciliate a covetous man by means of a gift, an obstinate man with folded hands in salutation, a fool by humouring him, and a learned man by truthful words.

112. It is better to be without a kingdom than to rule over a petty one; better to be without a friend than to befriend a rascal; better to be without a disciple than to have a stupid one; and better to be without a wife than to have a bad one.

113. How can people be made happy in a petty kingdom? What peace can we expect from a rascal friend? What happiness can we have at home in the company of a bad wife? How can renown be gained by instructing an unworthy disciple?

114. Learn one thing from a lion; one from a crane; four a cock; five from a crow; six from a dog; and three from an ass.

115. The one excellent thing that can be learned from a lion is that whatever a man intends doing should be done by him with a whole-hearted and strenuous effort.

116. The wise man should restrain his senses like the crane and accomplish his purpose with due knowledge of his place, time and ability.

117. To wake at the proper time; to take a bold stand and fight; to make a fair division (of property) among relations; and to earn one's own bread by personal exertion are the four excellent things to be learned from a cock.

118. Union in privacy (with one's wife); boldness; storing away useful items; watchfulness; and not easily trusting others; these five things are to be learned from a crow.

119. Contentment with little or nothing to eat although one may have a great appetite; to awaken instantly although one may be in a deep slumber; unflinching devotion to the master; and bravery; these six qualities should be learned from the dog.

120. Although an ass is tired, he continues to carry his burden; he is unmindful of cold and heat; and he is always contented; these three things should be learned from the ass.

121. He who shall practice these twenty virtues shall become invincible in all his undertakings.

122. A wise man should not reveal his loss of wealth, the vexation of his mind, the misconduct of his own wife, base words spoken by others, and disgrace that has befallen him.

123. He who gives up shyness in monetary dealings, in acquiring knowledge, in eating and in business, becomes happy.

124. The happiness and peace attained by those satisfied by the nectar of spiritual tranquillity is not attained by greedy persons restlessly moving here and there.

125. One should feel satisfied with the following three things; his own wife, food given by Providence and wealth acquired by honest effort; but one should never feel satisfied with the following three; study, chanting the holy names of the Lord (japa) and charity.

126. Do not pass between two Brahmanas, between a Brahmana and his sacrificial fire, between a wife and her husband, a master and his servant, and a plough and an ox.

127. Do not let your foot touch fire, the spiritual master or a Brahmana; it must never touch a cow, a virgin, an old person or a child.

128. Keep one thousand cubits away from an elephant, a hundred from a horse, ten from a horned beast, but keep away from the wicked by leaving the country.

129. An elephant is controlled by a goad (ankusha), a horse by a slap of the hand, a horned animal with the show of a stick, and a rascal with a sword.

130. Brahmanas find satisfaction in a good meal, peacocks in the peal of thunder, a sadhu in seeing the prosperity of others, and the wicked in the misery of others.

131. Conciliate a strong man by submission, a wicked man by opposition, and the one whose power is equal to yours by politeness or force.

132. The power of a king lies in his mighty arms; that of a Brahmana in his spiritual knowledge; and that of a woman in her beauty youth and sweet words.

133. Do not be very upright in your dealings for you would see by going to the forest that straight trees are cut down while crooked ones are left standing.

134. Swans live wherever there is water, and leave the place where water dries up; let not a man act so– and come and go as he pleases.

135. Accumulated wealth is saved by spending just as incoming fresh water is saved by letting out stagnant water.

136. He who has wealth has friends and relations; he alone survives and is respected as a man.

137. The following four characteristics of the denizens of heaven may be seen in the residents of this earth planet; charity, sweet words, worship of the Supreme Personality of Godhead, and satisfying the needs of Brahmanas.

138. The following qualities of the denizens of hell may characterise men on earth; extreme wrath, harsh speech, enmity with one's relations, the company with the base, and service to men of low extraction.

139. By going to the den of a lion pearls from the head of an elephant may be obtained; but by visiting the hole of a jackal nothing but the tail of a calf or a bit of the hide of an ass may found.

140. The life of an uneducated man is as useless as the tail of a dog which neither covers its rear end, nor protects it from the bites of insects.

141. Purity of speech, of the mind, of the senses, and the of a compassionate heart are needed by one who desires 6to rise to the divine platform.

142. As you seek fragrance in a flower, oil in the sesamum seed, fire in wood, ghee in milk, and jaggery (guda) in sugarcane; so seek the spirit that is in the body by means of discrimination.

143. Low class men desire wealth; middle class men both wealth and respect; but the noble, honour only; hence honour is the noble man's true wealth.

144. The lamp eats up the darkness and therefore it produces lamp black; in the same way according to the nature of our diet (sattva, rajas, or tamas) we produce offspring in similar quality.

145. O wise man! Give your wealth only to the worthy and never to others. The water of the sea received by the clouds is always sweet. The rain water enlivens all living beings of the earth both movable (insects, animals, humans, etc.) and immovable (plants, trees, etc.), and then returns to the ocean it value multiplied a million fold.

146. The wise who discern the essence of things have declared that the yavana (meat eater) is equal in baseness to a thousand candalas the lowest class), and hence a yavana is the basest of men; indeed there is no one more base.

147. After having rubbed oil on the body, after encountering the smoke from a funeral pyre, after sexual intercourse, and after being shaved, one remains a chandala until he bathes.

148. Water is the medicine for indigestion; it is invigorating when the food that is eaten is well digested; it is like nectar when drunk in the middle of a dinner; and it is like poison when taken at the end of a meal.

149. Knowledge is lost without putting it into practice; a man is lost due to ignorance; an army is lost without a commander; and a woman is lost without a husband.

150. A man who encounters the following three is unfortunate; the death of his wife in his old age, the entrusting of money into the hands of relatives, and depending upon others for food.

151. Chanting of the Vedas without making ritualistic sacrifices to the Supreme Lord through the medium of Agni, and sacrifices not

followed by bountiful gifts are futile. Perfection can be achieved only through devotion (to the Supreme Lord) for devotion is the basis of all success.

152. There is no austerity equal to a balanced mind, and there is no happiness equal to contentment; there is no disease like covetousness, and no virtue like mercy.

153. Anger is a personification of Yama (the demigod of death); thirst is like the hellish river Vaitarani; knowledge is like a kamadhenu (the cow of plenty); and contentment is like Nandanavana (the garden of Indra).

154. Moral excellence is an ornament for personal beauty; righteous conduct, for high birth; success for learning; and proper spending for wealth.

155. Beauty is spoiled by an immoral nature; noble birth by bad conduct; learning, without being perfected; and wealth by not being properly utilised.

156. Water seeping into the earth is pure; and a devoted wife is pure; the king who is the benefactor of his people is pure; and pure is the Brahmana who is contented.

157. Discontented Brahmanas, contented kings, shy prostitutes, and immodest housewives are ruined.

158. Of what avail is a high birth if a person is destitute of scholarship? A man who is of low extraction is honoured even y the demigods if he is learned.

159. A learned man is honoured by the people. A learned man commands respect everywhere for his learning. Indeed, learning is honoured everywhere.

160. those who are endowed with beauty and youth and who are born of noble families are worthless if they have no learning. They are just like the kimshuka blossoms ( f lowers of the palasa tree) which, though beautiful, have no fragrance.

161. The earth is encumbered with the weight of the f lesh-eaters, wine-bibblers, dolts and blockheads, who are beasts in the form of men.

162. There is no enemy like a yajna (sacrifice) which consumes the kingdom when not attended by feeding on a large scale; consumes the priest when the chanting is not done properly; and consumes the yajaman (the responsible person) when the gifts are not made.

163. My dear child, if you desire to be free from the cycle of birth and death, then abandon the objects of sense gratification as poison. Drink instead the nectar of forbearance, upright conduct, mercy, cleanliness and truth.

164. Those base men who speak of the secret faults of others destroy themselves like serpents who stray onto anthills.

165. Perhaps nobody has advised Lord Brahma, the creator, to impart perfume to gold; fruit to the sugarcane; f lowers to the sandalwood tree; wealth to the learned; and long life to the king.

166. Nectar (amrita) is the best among medicines; eating good food is the best of all types of material happiness; the eye is the chief among all organs; and the head occupies the chief position among all parts of the body.

167. No messenger can travel about in the sky and no tidings come from there. The voice of its inhabitants as never heard, nor can any contact be established with 7them. Therefore the Brahmana who predicts the eclipse of the sun and moon which occur in the sky must be considered as a vidwan (man of great learning).

168. The student, the servant, the traveller, the hungry person, the frightened man, the treasury guard, and the steward: these seven ought to be awakened if they fall asleep.

169. The serpent, the king, the tiger, the stinging wasp, the small child, the dog owned by other people, and the fool: these seven ought not to be awakened from sleep.

170. Of those who have studied the Vedas for material rewards, and those who accept foodstuffs offered by shudras, what potency have they? They are just like serpents without fangs.

171. He who neither rouses fear by his anger, nor confers a favour when he is pleased can neither control nor protect. What can he do?

172. The serpent may, without being poisonous, raise high its hood, but the show of terror is enough to frighten people– whether he be venomous or not.

173. Wise men spend their mornings in discussing gambling, the afternoon discussing the activities of women, and the night hearing about the activities of theft. (The f irst item above refers to the gambling of King Yuddhisthira, the great devotee of Krishna. The second item refers to the glorious deeds of mother Sita, the consort of Lord Ramachandra. The third item hints at the adorable childhood pastimes of Sri Krishna who stole butter from the elderly cowherd ladies of Gokula. Hence Chanakya Pandita advises wise persons to spend the morning absorbed in Mahabharata, the afternoon studying Ramayana, and the evening devotedly hearing the Srimad-Bhagvatam.)

174. By preparing a garland for a Deity with one's own hand; by grinding sandal paste for the Lord with one's own hand; and by writing sacred texts with one's own hand– one becomes blessed with opulence equal to that of Indra.

175. Poverty is set off by fortitude; shabby garments by keeping them clean; bad food by warming it; and ugliness by good behaviour.

176. One destitute of wealth is not destitute, he is indeed rich (if he is learned); but the man devoid of learning is destitute in every way.

177. We should carefully scrutinise that place upon which we step (having it ascertained to be free from filth and living creatures like insects, etc.); we should drink water which has been filtered (through a clean cloth); we should speak only those words which have the sanction of the satras; and do that act which we have carefully considered.

178. He who desires sense gratification must give up all thoughts of acquiring knowledge; and he who seeks knowledge must not hope for sense gratification. How can he who seeks sense gratification acquire knowledge, and he who possesses knowledge enjoy mundane sense pleasure?

179. What is it that escapes the observation of poets? What is that act women are incapable of doing? What will drunken people not prate? What will not a crow eat?

180. Fate makes a beggar a king and a king a beggar. He makes a rich man poor and a poor man rich.

181. The beggar is a miser's enemy; the wise counsellor is the fool's enemy; her husband is an adulterous wife's enemy; and the moon is the enemy of the thief.

182. Those who are destitute of learning, penance, knowledge, good disposition, virtue and benevolence are brutes wandering the earth in the form of men. They are burdensome to the earth.

183. Those that are empty-minded cannot be benefited by instruction. Bamboo does not acquire the quality of sandalwood by being associated with the Malaya Mountain.

184. What good can the scriptures do to a man who has no sense of his own? Of what use is as mirror to a blind man?

185. Nothing can reform a bad man, just as the posterious cannot become a superior part of the body though washed one hundred times.

186. By offending a kinsman, life is lost; by offending others, wealth is lost; by offending the king, everything is lost; and by offending a Brahmana one's whole family is ruined.

187. It is better to live under a tree in a jungle inhabited by tigers and elephants, to maintain oneself in such a place with ripe fruits and spring water, to lie down on grass and to wear the ragged barks of trees than to live amongst one's relations when reduced to poverty.

188. The Brahmana is like tree; his prayers are the roots, his chanting of the Vedas are the branches, and his religious act are the leaves.

Consequently effort should be made to preserve his roots for if the roots are destroyed there can be no branches or leaves.

189. My mother is Kamala Devi (Lakshmi), my father is Lord Janardana (Vishnu), my kinsmen are the Vishnubhaktas (Vaisnavas) and, my homeland is all the three worlds.

190. (Through the night) a great many kinds of birds perch on a tree but in the morning they fly in all the ten directions. Why should we lament for that? (Similarly, we should not grieve when we must inevitably part company from our dear ones).

191. He who possesses intelligence is strong; how can the man that is unintelligent be powerful? The elephant 8of the forest having lost his senses by intoxication was tricked into a lake by a small rabbit. This verse refers to a famous story from the niti-sastra called pancatantra compiled by the pandit Vishnusharma 2500 years ago.

192. Why should I be concerned for my maintenance while absorbed in praising the glories of Lord Vishwambhara (Vishnu), the supporter of all? Without the grace of Lord Hari, how could milk flow from a mother's breast for a child's nourishment? Repeatedly thinking only in this way, O Lord of the Yadus, O husband of Lakshmi, all my time is spent in serving Your lotus feet.

193. Generosity, pleasing address, courage and propriety of conduct are not acquired, but are inbred qualities.

194. He who forsakes his own community and joins another perishes as the king who embraces an unrighteous path.

195. The elephant has a huge body but is controlled by the ankusha (goad): yet, is the goad as large as the elephant? Alighted candle banishes darkness: is the candle as vast as the darkness. A mountain is broken even by a thunderbolt: is the thunderbolt therefore as big as the mountain? No, he whose power prevails is really mighty; what is there in bulk?

196. He who is engrossed in family life will never acquire knowledge; there can be no mercy in the eater of flesh; the greedy man will not be truthful; and purity will not be found in a woman a hunter.

197. The wicked man will not attain sanctity even if he is instructed in different ways, and the nim tree will not become sweet even if it is sprinkled from the top to the roots with milk and ghee.

198. Mental dirt cannot be washed away even by onehundred baths in the sacred waters, just as a wine pot cannot be purified even by evaporating all the wine by f ire.

199. It is not strange if a man reviles a thing of which he has no knowledge, just as a wild hunter's wife throws away the pearl that is found in the head of an elephant, and picks up a gunj(a type of seed which poor tribals wear as ornaments).

200. He who for one year eats his meals silently (inwardly meditating upon the Lord's prasadam); attains to the heavenly planets for a thousand crore of years. ( Note: one crore equals ten million)

201. The student (brahmacari) should completely renounce the following eight things— his lust, anger, greed, desire for sweets, sense of decorating the body, excessive curiosity, excessive sleep, and excessive endeavour for bodily maintenance.

202. He alone is a true Brahmana (dvija or "twice-born") who is satisfied with one meal a day, who has the six samskaras (or acts of purification such as garbhadhana, etc.) performed for him, and who cohabits with his wife only once in a month on an auspicious day after her menses.

203. The Brahmana who is engrossed in worldly affairs, brings up cows and is engaged in trade is really called a vaishya.

204. The Brahmana who deals in lac-die, articles, oil, indigo, silken cloth, honey, clarified butter, liquor, or flesh is called a shudra.

205. The Brahmana who thwarts the doings of others, who is hypocritical, selfish, and a deceitful hater, and while speaking mildly cherishes cruelty in his heart, is called a cat.

206. The Brahmana who destroys a pond, a well, a tank, a garden and a temple is called a mleccha.

207. The Brahmana who steals the property of the Deities and the spiritual preceptor, who cohabits with another's wife, and who maintains himself by eating anything and everything s called a chandala.

208. The meritorious should give away in charity all that they have in excess of their needs. By charity only Karna, Bali and King Vikramaditya survive even today. Just see the plight of the honeybees beating their legs in despair upon the earth. They are saying to themselves, "Alas! We neither enjoyed our stored-up honey nor gave it in charity, and now someone has taken it from us in an instant."

209. He is a blessed grihasta (householder) in whose house there is a blissful atmosphere, whose sons are talented, whose wife speaks sweetly, whose wealth is enough to satisfy his desires, who finds pleasure in the company of his wife, whose servants are obedient, in whose house hospitality is shown, the auspicious Supreme Lord is worshiped daily, delicious food and drink is partaken, and who finds joy in the company of devotees.

210. One whodevotedly gives a little to a Brahmana who is in distress is recompensed abundantly. Hence, O Prince, what is given to a good Brahmana is got back not in an equal quantity, but in an infinitely higher degree.

211. Those men who are happy in this world, who are generous towards their relatives, kind to strangers, indifferent to the wicked, loving to the good, shrewd in their dealings with the base, frank with the learned, courageous with enemies, humble with elders and stern with the wife.

212. O jackal, leave aside the body of that man at once, whose hands have never given in charity, whose ears have 9not heard the voice of learning, whose eyes have not beheld a pure devotee of the Lord, whose feet have never traversed to holy places, whose belly is filled with things obtained by crooked practices, and whose head is held high in vanity. Do not eat it, O jackal, otherwise you will become polluted.

213. "Shame upon those who have no devotion to the lotus feet of Sri Krishna, the son of mother Yasoda; who have no attachment for the describing the glories of Srimati Radharani; whose ears are not eager to listen to the stories of the Lord's lila." Such is the exclamation of the mridanga sound of dhik-tam dhik-tam dhigatam at kirtana.

214. What fault of spring that the bamboo shoot has no leaves? What fault of the sun if the owl cannot see during the daytime? Is it the fault of the clouds if no raindrops fall into the mouth of the chatak bird? Who can erase what Lord Brahma has inscribed upon our foreheads at the time of birth?

215. A wicked man may develop saintly qualities in the company of a devotee, but a devotee does not become impious in the company of a wicked person. The earth is scented by a flower that falls upon it, but the flower does not contact the odour of the earth.

216. One indeed becomes blessed by having darshan of a devotee; for the devotee has the ability to purify immediately, whereas the sacred tirtha gives purity only after prolonged contact.

Section-3

217. A stranger asked a Brahmana, "Tell me, who is great in this city?" The Brahmana replied, "The cluster of palmyra trees is great." Then the traveller asked, "Who is the most charitable person?" The Brahmana answered, "The washerman who takes the clothes in the morning and gives them back in the evening is the most charitable." He then asked, "Who is the ablest man?" The Brahmana answered, "Everyone is expert in robbing others of their wives and wealth." The man then asked the Brahmana, "How do you manage to live in such a city?" The Brahmana replied, "As a worm survives while even in a filthy place so do I survive here!"

218. The house in which the lotus feet of Brahmanas are not washed, in which Vedic mantras are not loudly recited, and in which the holy rites of svaha (sacrificial offerings to the Supreme Lord) and swadha (offerings to the ancestors) are not performed, is like a crematorium.

219. (It is said that a sadhu, when asked about his family, replied thusly): truth is my mother, and my father is spiritual knowledge; righteous conduct is my brother, and mercy is my friend, inner peace is my wife, and forgiveness is my son: these six are my kinsmen.

220. Our bodies are perishable, wealth is not at all permanent and death is always nearby. Therefore we must immediately engage in acts of merit.

221. Arjuna says to Krishna. "Brahmanas find joy in going to feasts, cows find joy in eating their tender grass, wives find joy in the company of their husbands, and know, O Krishna, that in the same way I rejoice in battle.

222. He who regards another's wife as his mother, the wealth that does not belong to him as a lump of mud, and the pleasure and pain of all other living beings as his own– truly sees things in the right perspective, and he is a true pandit.

223. O Raghava, the love of virtue, pleasing speech, and an ardent desire for performing acts of charity, guileless dealings with friends, humility in the guru's presence , deep tranquillity of mind, pure conduct, discernment of virtues, realised knowledge of the sastras, beauty of form and devotion to God are all found in you." (The great sage Vasistha Muni, the spiritual preceptor of the dynasty of the sun, said this to Lord Ramachandra at the time of His proposed coronation).

224. The desire tree is wood; the golden Mount Meru is motionless; the wish-fulfilling gem cintamani is just a stone; the sun is scorching; the moon is prone to wane; the boundless ocean is saline; the demigod of lust lost his body (due to Shiva's wrath); Bali Maharaja, the son of Diti, was born into a clan of demons; and Kamadhenu (the cow of heaven) is a mere beast. O Lord of the Raghu dynasty! I cannot compare you to any one of these (taking their merits into account).

225. Realised learning (vidya) is our friend while travelling , the wife is a friend at home, medicine is the friend of a sick man, and meritorious deeds are the friends at death.

226. Courtesy should be learned from princes, the art of conversation from pandits, lying should be learned from gamblers and deceitful ways should be learned from women.

227. The unthinking spender, the homeless urchin, the quarrel monger, the man who neglects his wife and is heedless in his actions– all these will soon come to ruination.

228. The wise man should not be anxious about his food; he should be anxious to be engaged only in dharma. The food of each man is created for him at his birth.

229. He, who is not shy in the acquisition of wealth, grain and knowledge, and in taking his meals, will be happy.

230. As centesimal droppings will fill a pot so also are knowledge, virtue and wealth gradually obtained.

231. The man who remains a fool even in advanced age is really a fool, just as the Indra-Varuna fruit does not become sweet no matter how ripe it might become.

232. A man may live but for a moment, but that moment should be spent in doing auspicious deeds. It is useless 10living even for a kalpa (4,320,000,000 years) and bringing only distress upon the two worlds (this world and the next).

233. We should not fret for what is past, nor should we be anxious about the future; men of discernment deal only with the present moment.

234. It certainly is nature of the demigods, men of good character, and parents to be easily pleased. Near and distant relatives are pleased when they are hospitably received with bathing, food, and drink; and pandits are pleased with an opportunity for giving spiritual discourse.

235 Even as the unborn babe is in the womb of his mother, these five are fixed as his life destiny: his life span, his activities, his acquisition of wealth and knowledge, and his time of death.

236. O see what a wonder it is! The doings of the great are strange: they treat wealth as light as a straw, yet, when they obtain it, they bend under its weight.

237. He who is overly attached to his family members experience fear and sorrow, for the root of all grief is attachment. Thus one should discard attachment to be happy.

238. He who is prepared for the future and he who deals cleverly with any situation that may arise are both happy; but the fatalistic man who wholly depends on luck is ruined.

239. If the king is virtuous, then the subjects are also virtuous. If the king is sinful, then the subjects also become sinful. If he is mediocre, then the subjects are mediocre. The subjects follow the example of the king. In short, as is the king so are the subjects.

240. I consider him who does not act religiously as dead though living, but he who dies acting religiously unquestionably lives long though he is dead.

241. He who has acquired neither virtue, wealth, satisfaction of desires nor salvation (dharma, artha, kama, moksa), lives an utterly useless life, like the "nipples" hanging from the neck of a goat.

242. The hearts of base men burn before the fire of other's fame, and they slander them being themselves unable to rise to such a high position.

243. Excessive attachment to sense pleasures leads to bondage, and detachment from sense pleasures leads to liberation; therefore it is the mind alone that is responsible for bondage or liberation.

244. He who sheds bodily identification by means of knowledge of the indwelling Supreme Self (Paramatma), will always be absorbed in meditative trance (samadhi) wherever his mind leads him.

245. Who realises all the happiness he desires? Everything is in the hands of God. Therefore one should learn contentment.

246. As a calf follows its mother among a thousand cows, so the (good or bad) deeds of a man follow him.

247. He whose actions are disorganised has no happiness either in the midst of men or in a jungle– in the midst of men his heart burns by social contacts, and his helplessness burns him in the forest.

248. As the man who digs obtains underground water by use of a shovel, so the student attains the knowledge possessed by his preceptor through his service.

249. Menreap the fruits of their deeds, and intellects bear the mark of deeds performed in previous lives; even so the wise act after due circumspection.

250. Even the man who has taught the spiritual significance of just one letter ought to be worshiped. He who does not give reverence to such a guru is born as a dog a hundred times, and at last takes birth as a chandala (dog-eater).

251. At the end of the yuga, Mount Meru may be shaken; at the end of the kalpa, the waters of the seven oceans may be disturbed; but a sadhu will never swerve from the spiritual path.

252. There are three gems upon this earth; food, water, and pleasing words– fools (mudhas) consider pieces of rocks as gems.

253. Poverty, disease, sorrow, imprisonment and other evils are the fruits borne by the tree of one's own sins.

254. Wealth, a friend, a wife, and a kingdom may be regained; but this body when lost may never be acquired again.

255. The enemy can be overcome by the union of large numbers, just as grass through its collectiveness wards off erosion caused by heavy rainfall.

256. Oil on water, a secret communicated to a base man, a gift given to a worthy receiver, and scriptural instruction given to an intelligent man spread out by virtue of their nature.

257. If men should always retain the state of mind they experience when hearing religious instruction, when present at a crematorium ground, and when in sickness– then who could not attain liberation.

258. If a man should feel before, as he feels after, repentance– then who would not attain perfection?

259. We should not feel pride in our charity, austerity, valour, scriptural knowledge, modesty and morality for the world is full of the rarest gems.

260. He who lives in our mind is near though he may actually be far away; but he who is not in our heart is far though he may really be nearby.

261. We should always speak what would please the man of whom we expect a favour, like the hunter who sings sweetly when he desires to shoot a deer.

262. It is ruinous to be familiar with the king, fire, the 11religious preceptor, and a woman. To be altogether indifferent of them is to be deprived of the opportunity to benefit ourselves, hence our association with them must be from a safe distance.

263. We should always deal cautiously with fire, water, women, foolish people, serpents, and members of a royal family; for they may, when the occasion presents itself, at once bring about our death.

264. He should be considered to be living who is virtuous and pious, but the life of a man who is destitute of religion and virtues is void of any blessing.

265. If you wish to gain control of the world by the performance of a single deed, then keep the following fifteen, which are prone to wander here and there, from getting the upper hand of you: the five sense objects (objects of sight, sound, smell, taste, and touch); the five sense organs (ears, eyes, nose, tongue and skin) and organs of activity (hands, legs, mouth, genitals and anus).

266. He is a pandit (man of knowledge) who speaks what is suitable to the occasion, who renders loving service according to his ability, and who knows the limits of his anger.

267 One single object (a woman) appears in three different ways: to the man who practices austerity it appears as a corpse, to the sensual it appears as a woman, and to the dogs as a lump of flesh.

268. A wise man should not divulge the formula of a medicine which he has well prepared; an act of charity which he has performed; domestic conflicts; private affairs with his wife; poorly prepared food he may have been offered; or slang he may have heard.

269. The cuckoos remain silent for a long time (for several seasons) until they are able to sing sweetly (in the Spring) so as to give joy to all.

270. We should secure and keep the following: the blessings of meritorious deeds, wealth, grain, the words of the spiritual master, and rare medicines. Otherwise life becomes impossible.

271. Eschew wicked company and associate with saintly persons. Acquire virtue day and night, and always meditate on that which is eternal forgetting that which is temporary.

272. For one whose heart melts with compassion for all creatures; what is the necessity of knowledge, liberation, matted hair on the head, and smearing the body with ashes.

273. There is no treasure on earth the gift of which will cancel the debt a disciple owes his guru for having taught him even asingle letter ( that leads to Krishna consciousness).

274. There are two ways to get rid of thorns and wicked persons; using footwear in the first case and in the second shaming them so that they cannot raise their faces again thus keeping them at a distance.

275. He, who wears unclean garments, has dirty teeth, as a glutton, speaks unkindly and sleeps after sunrise— although he may be the greatest personality— will lose the favour of Lakshmi.

276. He who loses his money is forsaken by his friends, his wife, his servants and his relations; yet when he regains his riches those who have forsaken him come back to him. Hence wealth is certainly the best of relations.

277. Sinfully acquired wealth may remain for ten years; in the eleventh year it disappears with even the original stock.

278. A bad action committed by a great man is not censured (as there is none that can reproach him), and a good action performed by a low-class man comes to be condemned (because none respects him). Just see: the drinking of nectar is excellent, but it became the cause of Rahu's demise; and the drinking of poison is harmful, but when Lord Shiva (who is exalted) drank it, it became an ornament to his neck (nila-kanta).

279. A true meal is that which consists of the remnants left after a Brahmana's meal. Love which is shown to others is true love, not that which is cherished for one's own self. to abstain from sin is true wisdom. That is an act of charity which is performed without ostentation.

280. For want of discernment the most precious jewels lie in the dust at the feet of men while bits of glass are worn on their heads. But we should not imagine that the gems have sunk in value, and the bits of glass have risen in importance. When a person of critical judgement shall appear, each will be given its right position.

281. Sastric knowledge is unlimited, and the arts to be learned are many; the time we have is short, and our opportunities to learn are beset with obstacles. Therefore select for learning that which is most important, just as the swan drinks only the milk in water.

282. He is a chandala who eats his dinner without entertaining the stranger who has come to his house quite accidentally, having travelled from a long distance and is wearied.

283. One may know the four Vedas and the Dharmasastras, yet if he has no realisation of his own spiritual self, he can be said to be like the ladle which stirs all kinds of foods but knows not the taste of any.

284. Those blessed souls are certainly elevated who, while crossing the ocean of life, take shelter of a genuine Brahmana, who is likened unto a boat. They are unlike passengers aboard an ordinary ship which runs the risk of sinking.

285. The moon, who is the abode of nectar and the presiding deity of all medicines, although immortal like amrita and resplendent in form, loses the brilliance of his rays when he retires to the abode of the sun (day time). Therefore will not an ordinary man be made to feel inferior by going to live at the house of another?

286. This humble bee, who always resides among the soft petals of the lotus and drinks abundantly its sweet nectar, is now feasting on the flower of the ordinary kutaja. Being in a strange country where the lotuses do not exist, he is considering the pollen of the kutaja to be nice.

287. (Lord Vishnu asked His spouse Lakshmi why She did not care to live in the house of a Brahmana, when She replied) " O Lord a rishi named Agastya drank up My father (the ocean) in anger; Brighu Muni kicked You; Brahmanas pride themselves on their learning having sought the favour of My competitor Sarasvati; and lastly they pluck each day the lotus which is My abode, and therewith worship Lord Shiva. Therefore, O Lord, I fear to dwell with a Brahmana and that properly.

288. There are many ways of binding by which one can be dominated and controlled in this world, but the bond of affection is the strongest. For example, take the case of the humble bee which, although expert at piercing hardened wood, becomes caught in the embrace of its beloved flowers (as the petals close at dusk).

289. Although sandalwood is cut, it does not forsake its natural quality of fragrance; so also the elephant does not give up sportiveness though he should grow old. The sugarcane does not cease to be sweet though squeezed in a mill; so the man of noble extraction does not lose his lofty qualities, no matter how pinched he is by poverty.

290. The heart of a woman is not united; it is divided. While she is talking with one man, she looks lustfully at another and thinks fondly of a third in her heart.

291. The fool (mudha) who fancies that a charming young lady loves him, becomes her slave and he dances like a shakuntal bird tied to a string.

292. Who is there who, having become rich, has not become proud? What licentious man has put an end to his calamities? What man in this world has not been overcome by a woman? Who is always loved by the king? Who is there who has not been overcome by the ravages of time? What beggar has attained glory? Who has become happy by contracting the vices of the wicked?

293. A man attains greatness by his merits, not simply by occupying an exalted seat. Can we call a crow an eagle (garuda) simply because he sits on the top of a tall building?

294. The man who is praised by others as great is regarded as worthy though he may be really void of all merit. But the man who sings his own praises lowers himself in the estimation of others though he should be Indra (the possessor of all excellences).

295. If good qualities should characterise a man of discrimination, the brilliance of his qualities will be recognised just as a gem which is essentially bright really shines when fixed in an ornament of gold.

296. Even one whobyhisqualities appears to be all knowing suffers without patronage; the gem, though precious, requires a gold setting.

297. I do not deserve that wealth which is to be attained by enduring much suffering, or by transgressing the rules of virtue, or by flattering an enemy.

298. Those who were not satiated with the enjoyment of wealth, food and women have all passed away; there are others now passing away who have likewise remained unsatiated; and in the future still others will pass away feeling themselves unsatiated.

299. All charities and sacrifices (performed for fruitive gain) bring only temporary results, but gifts made to deserving persons (those who are Krishna consciousness) and protection offered to all creatures shall never perish.

300. A blade of grass is light, cotton is lighter, the beggar is infinitely lighter still. Why then does not the wind carry him away? Because it fears that he may ask alms of him.

301. It is better to die than to preserve this life by incurring disgrace. The loss of life causes but a moment's grief, but disgrace brings grief every day of one's life.

302. All the creatures are pleased by loving words; and therefore we should address words that are pleasing to all, for there is no lack of sweet words.

303. There are two nectarean fruits hanging from the tree of this world: one is the hearing of sweet words (such as Krishna-katha) and the other, the society of saintly men.

304. The good habits of charity, learning and austerity practised during many past lives continue to be cultivated in this birth by virtue of the link (yoga) of this present life to the previous ones.

305. Onewhoseknowledge is confined to books and whose wealth is in the possession of others, can use neither his knowledge nor wealth when the need for them arises.

306. The scholar who has acquired knowledge by studying innumerable books without the blessings of a bonafide spiritual master does not shine in an assembly of truly learned men just as an illegitimate child is not honoured in society.

307. We should repay the favours of others by acts of kindness; so also should we return evil for evil in which there is no sin, for it is necessary to pay a wicked man in his 13own coin.

308. That thing which is distant, that thing which appears impossible, and that which is far beyond our reach, can be easily attained through tapasya (religious austerity), for nothing can surpass austerity.

309. What vice could be worse than covetousness? What is more sinful than slander? For one who is truthful, what need is there for austerity? For one who has a clean heart, what is the need for pilgrimage? If one has a good disposition, what other virtue is needed? If a man has fame, what is the value of other ornamentation? What need is there for wealth for the man of practical knowledge? And if a man is dishonoured, what could there be worse in death?

310. Though the sea, which is the reservoir of all jewels, is the father of the conch shell, and the Goddess of fortune Lakshmi is conch's sister, still the conch must go from door to door for alms (in the hands of a beggar). It is true, therefore, that one gains nothing without having given in the past.

311. When a man has no strength left in him he becomes a sadhu, one without wealth acts like a brahmacari, a sick man behaves like a devotee of the Lord, and when a woman grows old she becomes devoted to her husband.

312. There is poison in the fang of the serpent, in the mouth of the fly and in the sting of a scorpion; but the wicked man is saturated with it.

313. The woman who fasts and observes religious vows without the permission of her husband shortens his life, and goes to hell.

314. A woman does not become holy by offering by charity, by observing hundreds of fasts, or by sipping sacred water, as by sipping the water used to wash her husband's feet.

315. The hand is not so well adorned by ornaments as by charitable offerings; one does not become clean by smearing sandalwood paste upon the body as by taking a bath; one does not become so much satisfied by dinner as by having respect shown to him; and salvation is not attained by self-adornment as by cultivation of spiritual knowledge.

316. The eating of tundi fruit deprives a man of his sense, while the vacha root administered revives his reasoning immediately. A woman at once robs a man of his vigour while milk at once restores it.

317. He who nurtures benevolence for all creatures within his heart overcomes all difficulties and will be the recipient of all types of riches at every step.

318. What is there to be enjoyed in the world of Lord Indra for one whose wife is loving and virtuous, who possesses wealth, who has a well-behaved son endowed with good qualities, and who has a grandchildren born of his children?

319. Men have eating, sleeping, fearing and mating in common with the lower animals. That in which men excel the beasts is discretionary knowledge; hence, indiscreet men who are without knowledge should be regarded as beasts.

320. If the bees which seek the liquid oozing from the head of a lust-intoxicated elephant are driven away by the flapping of his ears, then the elephant has lost only the ornament of his head. The bees are quite happy in the lotus filled lake.

321. A king, a prostitute, Lord Yamaraja, fire, a thief, a young boy, and a beggar cannot understand the suffering of others. The eighth of this category is the tax collector.

322. O lady, why are you gazing downward? Has something of yours fallen on the ground? (She replies) O fool, can you not understand the pearl of my youth has slipped away?

323. O ketki flower! Serpents live in your midst, you bear no edible fruits, your leaves are covered with thorns, you are crooked in growth, you thrive in mud, and you are not easily accessible. Still for your exceptional fragrance you are as dear as kinsmen to others. Hence, a single excellence overcomes a multitude of blemishes.

# Chapter 2: Chanakya Sutram

Section-1

1. May the Great Goddess of Prosperity "Rajyashree" protect the functionaries of the State by giving them the correct dispositions.

2. The basis of "sukha" or all true pleasantness is "dharma" or righteous conduct.

3. The basis of all "dharma" is "artha" or wealth.

4. The basis of all "artha" is "rajya" or the State.

5. The basis for the stability of the State lies in control over the "indriya" or sense faculties providing pleasure.

6. The basis for control over the sensual faculties is in "vinay" or humility.

7. The basis for humility is devotion to those grown old through wisdom.

8. Through devotion to the wise, one attains proficiency with the maximum efficiency.

9. It is imperative for all the functionaries of the State to perform their duties with the maximum efficiency.

10. To perform State duties with the maximum efficiency, the functionaries of the State must learn to control their sensual needs, and maximise their internal potentials.

11. Those who have vanquished their baser selves may become prosperous naturally, can

retain their prosperity, and be successful in their endeavours.

12. The wealth and properties of the State naturally increases the level of prosperity of the people.

13. Where the people and the functionaries of the State follow sound moral principles, the State can function effectively even without a king.

14. Of all discords the anger of the people is the most to be feared. The basis for State functioning lies in the acceptance and good wishes of the people.

15. It is better not to have a king than to have one who is unworthy. Rather than have a king who is without truth and sound principles, who is greedy, selfish and tyrannical, the king- makers must run the affairs of the State themselves using democratic methods and following enlightened public opinion.

16. After filling himself with the right kingly qualities, the ruler of the State must select as assistants those talented individuals who are equally wise.

17. Without the intellectual assistance of his council of ministers it is not possible for the ruler to take the right decisions regarding his duties.

18. Just as there cannot be a one-wheeled chariot, there cannot be a king without a council of ministers.

19. The assistant who steadfastly adheres to the ruler, and is of equable temperament both in times of prosperity and adversity, is best.

20. The conscientious ruler must resolve complex issues by careful and thorough analysis of

the "for" and "against" sides, and including the consequences of his decisions. For help, he needs for ministers individuals who are famous, wise, prosperous, enthusiastic, impressive, hardy, hard working, well-intentioned, well-behaved; who truly love the ruling system and live in the land.

21. That minister should he held best, he who correctly assesses the gravity of a problem, and solves it with the maximum efficiency and use of imagination.

22. A minister is to be appointed if after showing his supremacy in debate and knowledge of laws, he also passes tests conducted secretly.

23. Tasks can be successfully executed only after thorough discussion and careful planning.

24. A task can be completed with success if information relating to the beneficial and non-

beneficial consequences of the task is kept secret.

25. Any sort of carelessness can upset the security issues involved in a task and so cause its ruination. A minister must be held totally responsible for the task under his supervision.

26. Any relaxation in security measures will cause knowledge of secret matters to pass into
the hands of the enemy.

27. Knowing that the enemy is always keen for secret information, and is on the lookout for disgruntled ministers who could give it, all doors that could create discord among ministers must be blocked.

28. Complete security for the ministers is necessary for the good of the State. 29. Since the minister gives dynamism to duty, the strength of the State lies in the continued existence and good health of the ministers.

30. As the lamp shows the path, so does the minister give direction to those afflicted by indecision.

31. For victory over foes, the ruler must know the full extents of their weaknesses. Only capable ministers can provide him with such information.

32. In the council of ministers, no one should try to force his views by drowning the views of others. A reasonable attitude must prevail.

33. Unanimity in the council of ministers leads to success in the realization of goals.

34. The ideal ministers are those who have amassed personal wealth through righteous conduct, have overcome selfish desires and have conscience.

35. If six ears listen to a secret executive decision, that becomes public knowledge.

36. Those who take the misfortunes upon others as misfortunes upon themselves are best suited to be friends.

37. By acquiring true friends, one gains strength.

38. The strong try to get advantages to which they have no right.

39. Giving even a little to the lazy does not protect material wealth.

40. Laziness deprives the State of strength, and labour increases the wealth of the State.

41. Without continued increase of wealth, the demise of the State is inevitable.

42. If the ruler out of laziness lets his servants do his work as the ruler, then disaster is certain.

43. If out of laziness the ruler does not do pilgrimage to centres of holiness, learning and experience, there can be no progress for the State.

44. The four basic tenets for the functioning of the State are: correct appointments of the State's functionaries; the State's functionaries must do nothing to decrease the growth of the wealth of the State; they must not indulge in wasteful expenditure; nor must they allow out of lack of use the waste of the wealth of the State.

45. The people of the State can have moral principles only when the workings of the State are based upon moral principles.

46. Knowledge of the duties owed to one's own State, and to the neighbouring States, in terms of the laws and principles involved, is an essential aspect of Statecraft.

47. Where the basic tenets for the functioning of the State are held sacred, there is prosperity and happiness for the State.

48. Constant surveillance of the enemies is essential for the security of the State. 49. Friendship or enmity with neighbouring States is just the way the world works.

50. It is worthy for the king to follow the path of high principle.

51. The enemy can attack the State at any time.

52. Two warring States become friendly later.

53. One does not acquire either friends or enemies without reason.

54. It is the duty of the high-principled but weak ruler to make military alliances with a stronger and powerful State.

55. The high-principled ruler of a strong State must never make military alliances with unprincipled States.

56. There can be honourable military alliance between States having unequal powers, just as there can be no strong union between hot iron and cold iron.

57. The strong king should attack his enemy only when he finds the enemy weaker than himself.

58. The king must never fight another king of equal strength.

59. A weak army moves away from the powerful enemy as foot soldiers move away from those mounted upon elephants.

60. The ruler should act upon the information given him by his secret spies about every effort, initiative, political desire and treaties of his enemies.

61. The State can keep up its unique, dear and particular characteristics only when there is keen observation of the ways and actions of the neighbouring States, without reference to the nature of the alliances involved with them, whether friendly, or not.

62. It is imperative for the ruler to stamp out the terrorist actions in his State by enemy States, and to prevent the spies from friendly States to sow discord and division among his people.

63. A weak king should seek the protection of a powerful and principled monarch.

64. It is perilous to make any treaty with a ruler who is weak because of his lack of self-

confidence and incompetence.

65. Extreme caution must be taken while making treaties; or else the ruler may get burnt if parities are not maintained.

66. Rebellion against the State should not be done.

67. The ruler must not wear such rich garments that excite the envy of the population.

68. The people of the State must not aspire to the accoutrements of the legitimate ruler of the State.

69. The ruler should turn the envious and ambitious personalities, who aspire to his role, against each other, using requisite cleverness.

Dissension is more manageable when confined to small and mutually warring groups.

70. It is lack of desire that leads to incomplete or unsuccessful completion of tasks. Keen interest, resolve, proper conception and self-confidence: all result from desire.

71. A ruler who is governed by sensual pleasures is destroyed, no matter how powerful he may be.

72. Those, which are addicted to gambling, are unfit to execute the functions of the State.

73. Addiction to hunting is destructive to morality and wealth.

74. The wealth of the State increases when every person is given the right to acquire the goods that sustain life.

75. Those which are addicted to drinking are unfit to be trusted with important work.

76. Those who are infatuated by lust cannot execute any State-related task with full dedication, as they will not find it possible to concentrate upon the subtler aspects.

77. Harsh, cruel and uncouth words, spoken in public, produce more pain than fire. They result from a low and wicked mind, and increase the rage in the hearers, sowing the seeds of conflict.

78. The giver of justice should not be harsh with punishments. The nature of punishments should always be seen as consistent with the welfare of the State, and should have the support of the people of the State.

79. A miserly ruler, who simply sits upon his wealth and does not spend upon the needs of the State, ceases to create scope for increased revenues to the treasury, and therefore leads to the impoverishment of the State.

80. While wealth coming to the treasury through ugly external means appears welcome, in reality such wealth is destructive to the wealth generated locally.

81. When the ruler is lax with administering just punishments, he invites his enemies to become more powerful.

82. The security of the State depends upon the laws relating to punishments being correctly, impartially and efficiently administered.

83. The capacity to inflict punishment is the ultimate resource of the State.

84. Bad ministers are incapable of inflicting just punishments. Thus they corrupt the functioning of the State.

85. The safety of the ruler, and his people, depend upon how correctly the systems of punishments are administered.

86. Upon the personal safety of the ruler depends the safety of the people.

87. The growth or destruction of the individual depends upon the choices the individual may make about his behaviour.

88. Punishments should be given after careful consideration, and on a scientific basis.

89. The king must never be considered a weak, normal person, and neglected accordingly. He represents the full power and majesty of the State.

90. As the smallest of sparks can cause a huge forest fire, so can kingliness, even if present in minute measure, lead to enormous outcomes, when the will of the people is aligned with that of their ruler.

91. The righteous conduct and the fulfillment of the needs of the State depend on the stability of the revenue of the treasury.

92. How the State can do any work without resources?

93. If there are adequate resources with the state the work can be accomplished easily.

94. No work is difficult if it is done like worship.

95. If there is no adequate mobilisation of resources the work gets thwarted.

96. Means or resources are the true deputies of those who execute the work.

97. Once there are resources and executives, the targets to be achieved are clearly defined.

98. The destiny follows the systematic and result oriented efforts.

99. If destiny is adverse the responsibility nicely discharged fails to produce any tangible results.

100. Those which cease to take any efforts relying on destiny soon realise lack of resources to sustain life.

101. One should carefully consider about the necessity, the indipensibility, the outcome, the policy and the means and clear all the air of confusion. Once the confusion is cleared the task may be undertaken.

102. Once the work is started there should be no procrastination.

103. No work can be accomplished by the one who has unstable mind.

104. Those which don't make use of resources at hand ruin their work.

105. The work that is free of all defects is rare in the world.

106. One should not do a work where there is no certainty of any good outcome.

107. Those who are good at discerning the right time accomplish their work easily.

108. If the work is not done at the duty bound time the success of the work is devoured by time.

109. One should not delay discharging his duty by a single moment.

110. The work done at the right time and under the favorable conditions is successful.

111. Once the destiny becomes adverse the duties that could have been discharged very easily appear very tough.

112. Those which are pragmatic they should take care of both policy and implementation.

113. It is a rule that those who do the work at the right time get the success.

114. The ruler should use all techniques like giving honour, awards etc. and should cause accumulation of wealth in the State. These resources can be put to use when there is a need.

Section-2

115. Those who fail to understand the significance of the right time don't get any success.

116. One should decide on the basis of one's experience and analysis about how the work will be done. One should clearly define his duty in the work execution.

Aphorism117. One should be allocated that work for which he is competent.

Aphorism

He who is good at trouble shooting knows very well significant resources. He is good

at making the difficult tasks easy.

118. Those which are ignorant should not be given any credit even if they are successful. An ignorant, can't be successful. The success was just achieved accidentally.

119. The wood-eater ant by chance makes shapes of various articles. This is not a basis for his proficiency in making models of articles. Similarly if there is a person who behaves according to his own wish and lacks any power of discrimination and if he is able to do some work by chance he deserves no credit for the work.

120. People should come to know about the work only when the work is performed.

121. Sometimes work remains incomplete due to adverse conditions or human mistakes.

122. If there are natural calamities like earthquake, heavy rains, thunderstorms or internal disturbances or there is external aggression, the ruler should deal with the conditions by maintaining stability and peace of his intellect.

123. If the work is hampered by human factors, one should address these factors by using one's attentiveness and understanding.

124. Foolish people after they fail in the execution of the work repent for their mistakes which they should have corrected before starting the work. Or they blame others and say that someone else is responsible for the fiasco and they are not to be blamed. This is how they become faultless commentators.

125. One should not be lax in covering up one's weaknesses and identifying defects of the opponents. One should not unreasonably rely on anybody and never divulge one's secrets. If one doesn't behave like this disaster befalls one's nation.

126. A calf that feeds on mother's milk strikes breasts of a cow to get milk.

127. If one doesn't make full efforts for accomplishing the work, the work is aborted.

Aphorism 128. Beginning won't succeed in their work or they just sit idle without doing any work.

129. Those who shirk their responsibilities won't do anything for their dependants.

130. Those who can't see their duties with the eye of discretion are blind inspite of having eyes.

131. One should define one's duty taking into consideration the existing and future means.

132. Success forsake those who work without contemplation. Aphorism

Disaster should be removed by contemplation.

133. One should have complete and true understanding of one's strengths. One should not have any futile confidence about one's strengths.

134. Those who provide from their earning for their own people, brothers, guests, dependants, poor people, welfare organisations and

sustain themselves only on the remaining earnings, get the joy of eating nectar while they take their regular meals.

135. More avenues are opened for the resource mobilization of the state if the State performs it's duty in respect of land, wealth, commerce and arts.

136. Those who are fearful never have any thought of discharging any duty in their mind. They are good at identifying one excuse on the other for not doing anything.

137. Those who are appointed for doing work do their work or get their work done by others knowing the liking of the person who has provided them shelter.

138. As a calf gets milk from a cow in the way that is best for her nature, so does a person who serves the ruler performs his task of serving the State.

139. A person who is intelligent should not divulge secrets to the one who is foolish, without any ethics, who doesn't conform to any policy, base, indecisive.

140. Those who are unduly soft and who don't exercise any discretion in granting favors are not respected even by their own people.

141. The ruler who gives harsh punishment for small crimes invites hatred from all. He becomes a reason for creating disorder in his jurisdiction.

142. It is fair that the ruler should give reasonable punishment.

143. A person who is not serious doesn't get any recognition from people even if he is intelligent.

144. If a person is given too much responsibility he loses is enthusiasm and his work bears no fruits.

145. If a person starts accusing others in the State Assembly for settling his personal scores declares himself to be a culprit.

146. Those which are devoid of any manners and power of discrimination cause harm to their soul by their anger.

147. Those which are equipped with the wealth of truth are not devoid of anything that they desire.

148. Bravery alone won't help.

149. An addicted person can't perform his duty as he loses focus of his mind.

150. Procrastination invites an army of troubles.

151. It is better to die an uncertain death in a war than dying a certain death by shirking a war.

152. Those who keep wealth of others as the trustees of wealth, if they develop their selfish interest in the wealth and if they no more feel accountable to others for the wealth, will always try to serve their selfish interest.

153. Charity is a form of righteous conduct.

154. A person wastes his life if he lives like an ignorant person.

155. If a person indulges in petty desires he loses his righteousness and resources.

156. A person devoid of righteousness, rather who behaves exactly opposite to what he is supposed to renders his life useless. He causes instability in the society and disturbs the continuity of peace in the society.

157. He is a rare person in this world who is guileless and decent while dealing with a good person and who has his attention focused on performing his duties.

158. A good person while discharging his duty rejects prosperity that blemishes him as a blade of grass.

159. Even a single vice of a person makes many of his good qualities bad.

160. A good person who is always commited to truth guards the truth that seems a very difficult task on his own without relying on others.

161. A person should not do something that blemishes his character by succumbing to the vices like lust and anger. If he does so he may have a thorn pricking his heart forever.

162. As a lion never eats grass howsoever hungry may be against his habbit of being a non-vegetarian. So are the people who hold their character very high disregarding all excitement and disasters. They remain commited to truth, good character and glory.

163. A person should be commited to his credibility and duty to the State at the cost of his life.

164. Those who cause disputes among people on the basis of secrets known to them are deserted even by their family members.

165. If people who don't have any standing tell you something worthwhile you should listen to them.

166. Don't tell the truth to a person who is not eligible to know the truth, who derails the truth, who doesn't have any faith and who may find the truth bitter. If you do that you are offending the truth.

167. One should not disregard significant qualities of a person on seeing some common vice in him.

168. One may identify many defects in something good if one takes a gross view.

169. One may identify lack of shine, curves, oddness and may other defects in a gem stone. The best gemstone of the best class is not free from all defects. Similarly there could be some bodily and sensual disorders in intelligent people.

170. Those who don't abide by the social norms, those who don't listen to their conscience, those who don't abide by any limit should not be trusted upon.

171. If an enemy shows sweetness in his bahaviour that should be considered as hatred like a pot of poison having milk at the top.

172. Selfish people show humility if they want to serve their interest. So, one should discern true colours of such selfish people.

173. One should not behave contradictory to good people having experience.

174. He who is devoid of any quality becomes an abode of many qualities if he remains in contact with a man of qualities.

175. As water that takes shelter with milk mixes with milk fully, in the same way a person who surrenders to a man of qualities becomes similar to him.

176. The earth is devoid of fragrance but it gains fragrance when it comes in contact with a flower. Similarly a person who is devoid of qualities but capable of assimilation gains from a man of qualities if develops contact.

177. It is similar to silver acquiring status of gold when it is mixed therewith.

178. A foolish person due to defect of his intellect causes harm to his benefactor and serves his base interest.

179. A sinner is never afraid of being reviled.

180. An insurmountable enemy can be conquered by those who have enthusiasm.

181. The glory of knowledge is the resource of the ruler.

182. He who lacks enthusiasm, action and intellect can't get any success now or in future.

183. If there is lack of enthusiasm the success that is almost certain slips away. 184. He who wants fish has to go to dive in water and take the risk. Similarly a man of action should rise, run the risk of disaster, protect success in the form of his fate from all troubles and this is how he should accomplish his work.

185. One should never trust those who are not tested or who are not eligible for the work.

186. A poison is forever poison. It will never be nectar. As poison never changes it's form so does a man who is not trustworthy.

187. One should never take any help from enemies for doing the work.

188. One should never rely on the enemy for accomplishing one's objective.

189. One has relations with people only for attaining his objectives.

190. If an enemy's son is a friend one should protect him.

191. If you want to hit your enemy on his weak points and destroy him, you should continue to show him artificial honour and friendship until you identify his weak points.

192. The ruler who wants to emerge victorious should hit very hard the weak areas of his enemy.

193. The enemy should not know that the ruler is weak and the ruler should always appear strong to the enemy.

194. The enemy always attacks the areas which are assessed as weak.

195. The ruler should have no faith in the enemy who made friendly gestures but behaved like an enemy after the enemy is conquered.

196. The ruler who aspires to be victorious should use strong means to correct the wrong or ugly conduct of his own people.

197. When the ruler doesn't adhere to the good character and offends his own people intellectuals take his offence by heart.

198. A person as a whole becomes sick and incapacitated if any of his organ becomes sick. Similarly when any part of the ruling mechanism malfunctions it deprives the whole mechanism of its strengths.

199. Good conduct is the infallible means of defeating the enemy.

200. A mean person always demonstrates craftiness against good people.

201. One should not take any efforts to impart righteousness to a base, meek and foolish person.

202. One should not trust a cruel, foolish and mean person.

203. Even if you greet a bad person with magnanimity he will not miss any opportunity to harm you.

204. As a forest fire due to it's burning hot nature doesn't take any virtue from the sandalwood and burns it to ashes, a foolish person will always harm you disregarding all good done by you.

205. You should never offend any person.

206. One should always bear in mind that forgiveness is a great human quality. One should never cause any agony to those who deserve forgiveness.

207. Those which are devoid of intellect open the secrets that the ruler tells them in confidence.

208. Love is never expressed by words it is expressed by doing something in favour.

209. Only a resourceful person can issue any command.

210. A foolish person makes an obvious favour under the influence of something strange.

211. Those who lack discretion perish even when they are bestowed with royal affluence.

212. Those which lack patience don't get any happiness now or later.

213. In the absence of patience action becomes fruitless even though there was a certain capacity to get the results.

214. One needs to have patience if one wants to be successful.

215. The intelligent people shouldn't get too close to fools.

216. One should not have a glass of milk if that is offered by a person who has taken liquor.

217. The intellect should help one find a certain path to success when lot of difficulties arises.

218. A meal is conducive to good health if it is taken in limit.

219. If one has become sick after taking food that was not permissible, one should not take even the permissible food.

220. A person remains free from all diseases if he takes meals only when the earlier meal is digested and he feels hungry.

221. A sick person, an old person, a weak person should not ignore the worsening of any disease.

222. If a person is having improper digestion and still he takes meals that makes his stomach more sick and woeful.

223. A disease is worse than an enemy.

224. One should give charity on the basis of his capacity.

225. A person who is unreasonably cunning and greedy has a tendency to come very close and make relations.

226. Greed envelopes one's mind.

227. One should classify work on the basis of priority and do the work that has the highest priority.

228. If the work done by us or others derails we should verify where the problem has arisen and rectify the defect.

Section-3

229. An inhuman attack, a vile behaviour, not applying any intellect or showing unwanted bravery are in the very nature of a foolish person.

230. One should not exchange words with a fool.

231 One should not be good to a fool.

232.'Iron cuts iron' is the right policy that should be used against a fool.

233. It is very difficult for a fool to maintain relations.

234. Only the path of righteousness can protect a person.

235. A person can't get rid of his merits and demerits even when his body falls.

236. A person who shows mercy furthers his righteousness.

237. Righteousness gives rise to truth and charity.

238. A person who abides by righteousness can defeat the whole world.

239. The death that devours one and all can't perish the one who abides by righteousness.

240. Whenever the sin that reviles righteousness gains strength righteousness is done the highest offense.

241. Those devil people who revile the truth signal their destruction by reviling the truth.

242. The intellect that takes delight in unrighteousness signals doom.

243. A man who reviles others can't maintain secrecy of any matters.

244. One should not insist in knowing the secrets of others.

245. It is not in order that a ruler is dominated by unworthy followers.

246. One should not ignore one's well-wishers but one should take only that much care which they deserve.

247. One should disregard even one's mother if she is wicked.

248. As a part that gets infected is amputated, one should part with the kinsman who has turned inimical.

249. If a person is our benefactor he should be treated like a relative.

250. A medicine that cures a disease has to be obtained from a remote place like forest, similarly a benefactor should not be disregarded even if people consider him to be inferior.

251. One should never rely on what thieves say.

252. You should not ignore your enemy if he seems to be indifferent in his retaliatory attack.

253. A petty addiction may lead to one's total destruction.

254. A man thinks that he will live forever and he is always busy after things necessary for sustaining his life.

255. One who is wealthy commands respect on the basis of one's wealth.

256. Even if the Indra, The King of Heaven loses wealth he won't be respected anymore.

257. Poverty makes a living man a corpse.

258. One who is wealthy and gives donation becomes subject matter of everyone's interest even if he is ugly in his looks.

259. Those who are in need of money seek favour from a wealthy person knowing well that he is a miser.

260. The wealthy person who puts his wealth to social good though not belonging to a good family commands more respect compared to those who belong to good families but who don't do any social good.

261. A base person never fears that he may be offended or despised.

262. People who are pragmatic and clever don't bother about their livelihood.

263. He who controls his senses doesn't have any doubts of losing balance when he is exposed to the material world.

264. Those who know the secrets of life and have clarity about their duties don't fear death.

265. Good people want that wealth of others should also be put to noble use.

266. One should not look at wealth of others with an eye of greed.

267. If one looks at the wealth of others with an eye of greed, he may harm his social relations and may lead to his self-destruction.

268. One should not steal any wealth even as much as a blade of grass.

269. One who steals wealth of others causes destruction of his own wealth.

270. The noose of death is not as painful as that of poaching.

271. One need not steal anything to maintain one's life. One can maintain one's life with bare minimum things.

272. There is no need of any remedy after death.

273. The State should maintain it's supremacy under normal conditions.

274. Even good qualities of base people are applied for ulterior purpose.

275. A base person applies all his wisdom for doing base things so whatever wisdom is imparted to him becomes counter-productive.

276. There is nothing more useful than food for life.

277. There is no enemy of the State like scarcity of food or un-satiated hunger of people.

278. One who doesn't take any efforts, who is devoid of action and lazy is bound to die of starvation.

279. He who suffers from pangs of hunger doesn't consider anything to be unfit for eating.

280. He who puts his sense organs to unlimited use gets old earlier.

281. You should serve that master who considers no difference between his own life and the life of his people.

282. He whose master lacks sympathy thinks that he will get fire from a firefly.

283. One should serve that master who respects and discerns virtue.

284. Intercourse leads a man to his senility.

285. Intercourse leads a woman to her senility.

286. There should not be a marital bond between a base person and a great person.

287. There is no enemy greater than ego.

288. One should not offend one's enemy at a meeting and convert it from a place where thoughts prevail to a place where people hurt one another.

289. It is a pleasure to know that the enemy is not doing well.

290. A deprived person has no intellect or his intellect fails to deliver.

291. If a deprived person tells something beneficial none listens.

292. A man who doesn't have money to buy household necessities is offended by his wife.

293. As the Mango tree is left by the bees when its flowering season is over, everyone deserts a poor man as relationship with him doesn't offer any economic prospects.

294. Wisdom is the wealth of the poor.

295. As wisdom is stored internally and it is secret there is no possibility of any theft.

296. Wisdom widens the horizons of success.

297. A material body dies, the glory lives forever.

298. One who strives for the good of others is a good person.

299. If one says that he has gained knowledge from scriptures, he should demonstrate calmness of his senses.

300. The beacon of scriptures desists a person from doing anything wrong.

301. The wisdom of a base man is useless and should not be acquired.

302. One should not learn language of a base man.

303. One may learn commitment from a base person. Of course not the subject matter of commitment.

304. One should not ignore the virtue of a virtuous man by becoming intolerant.

305. One should learn virtue even from one's enemy.

306. One may extract nectar from poison if possible.

307. A person gets respect only under favourable conditions.

308. A man is respected only in the areas of his influence.

309. Those which are decorated with wisdom, humility, knowledge of scriptures, righteousness and knowledge are called as Arya, gentle, good.

310. One should never exceed the limit of good conduct.

311. One who has become good by the dint of one's lifelong penance can't be glorified by any title or material means.

312. There is no gem as valuable as a woman who adores her home.

314. Men of virtue are rare in this world.

315. If a person indulges in condemned actions he loses his status of being a human-being.

315. A person who is devoid of any action and who observes no self restraint doesn't have any right to study scriptures.

316. He who has no control over his sense organs can't abide by scriptures or can't be happy.

317. A man who observes no self restraint is not given any respect by his wife.

318. Only trees capable of flowering are offered water and not the dried trees.

319 Those who wish to grant favours prefers them who are good.

320. There is no possibility of getting any food by boiling sand. Similarly happiness is not created by foolish means.

321. People who have acquired great virtues should not be ridiculed.

322. One should remember that the cause effect relationship always prevails. So there can't be anything good from something bad.

323. The purpose of the work is more decisive than the constellation when the work is undertaken.

324. If some work is to be done urgently, there is no need to assess the constellation.

325. If someone becomes known to you well, his defects won't remain hidden.

326. A sinner judges others with his own standards and concludes that others are just like him.

327. It is very difficult to change one's disposition.

328. The penalty should be commensurate with the offense.

329. The answer should be commensurate with the query.

330. One should decorate one's exterior within one's economic means.

331. One's conduct should be compatible with one's family.

332. One's efforts should match the work that he has to do.

333. Donation should be made taking into account the eligibility of the donee.

334. One's robes should be compatible with one's state.

335. A servant should always favour his Master by his actions.

336. A wife should always favour her husband.

337. A disciple should always execute his preceptor's command.

338. A son should always follow his father's wishes.

339. If someone is doing unreasonable favour to you it would raise your suspicion.

340. If your master gets angry you should please him.

341. As a child that is beaten by his mother goes back to his mother and asks anything he wants from her only, so should one go back to one's people even if they seem to be harsh in their behaviour.

342. The elderly people who love you won't harm you by their anger.

Section-4

343. A foolish person can't see his own mistake and always finds faults with others.

344. Those who are cunning serve others with some ulterior motive.

345. These people have their own interest and their service is just a formality.

346. If a person known to you gives unjust favours that should arise your suspicion.

347. As a cow with some problem is better than thousand dogs, a servant without any formality is better than thousands who are set to decieve.

348. It is better to be contented with a small pigeon that you have today than a big pea-cock that you will have in future.

349. If any work is beset with immorality it corrupts the duty and defeats the purpose of the work.

350. He who is devoid of anger may conquer the whole world.

351. A progressive person due to lack of anger fortifies his intellect with his serious thinking.

352. You should not create conflicts with those who are intelligent, foolish, friends, preceptor and for whom your master uses kind words.

353. There can't be any prosperity without appropriating money belonging to others.

354. Those who chase money don't like taking any efforts for good things.

355. Those who depend on a vehicle lose their own speed.

356. A wife is a shackle that ties a man.

357. One should be deployed in that work which he knows well.

358. A harsh wife creates agony.

359. One should observe how his wife behaves.

360. One should not trust a woman.

361. A woman doesn't know the ways the world works and she lacks any stability of mind.

362. When all our teachers are ranked Mother occupies the first rank.

363. A son should always see that he meets all needs of his mother.

364. A man's intelligence gets covered by his dressing.

365. A restricted appearance is the embellishment for a woman.

366. The knowledge of Vedas is a true embellishment for Brahmins.

367. Truthfulness is the embellishment of all human-beings.

368. Wisdom paired with humility is the best of all embellishments.

369. One should live in a region that has no turbulence.

370. A region is fit for living where there is a majority of truthful good people.

371. One should not invite King's wrath.

372. There is no God greater than King.

373. The wrath of King is capable of burning those who revolt against him by reaching all corners of the State.

374. One should never go to a King with empty hands.

375. Similarly we should not go with empty hands to the preceptor and the one who is held in high esteem.

376. We should not become a subject of revile for those close to the royal family.

377. One should go often to the court of King.

378. One should be friendly to the ministers and friends of King.

379. One should not make personal relations with the women working for the King.

380. One should not see the King in his eyes.

381. A father feels great happiness when he has a son with virtue and good conduct.

382. Sons should be good at excelling all faculties of wisdom.

383. One should leave a village that turns hostile to the State.

384. One should leave a family and support his village if any such contradiction arises.

385. The birth of a son is the highest benefit.

386. A son protects his parents from calamities.

387. A good child by the dint of his wisdom, charity, status, honours and righteousness glorifies his family.

388. He who doesn't have a good son has no happiness.

389. A mother that gives birth to good children is a great wife.

390. Boys and girls should not mix with each other while learning.

391 A wife is not an object of sensual pleasure.

392. She is the nourisher of family and sustains infinite existence of family by giving birth to children.

393. One should not see a woman working at his house with a malicious intention.

394 One gets to a very low level by doing so.

395. A man who is all set for his doom disregards good advice offered by his well wishers.

396. One need not worry about his physical comforts.

397. Children chase their mother, happiness and sorrows follow the action that a man takes.

398. Good people always remember any small favour done to them always as if they were done a great favour.

399. A person who lacks all gratitude and eligibility should not be done any favour.

400. A person with malicious heart who has no gratitude just to release himself from the burden of gratitude turns hostile.

401. A good person never sits quiet unless he pays back the favour received.

402. One should never offend marks of divinity in any form.

403. The greatest light is one's eye-sight.

404. The vision of knowledge enables one to shun the wrong path.

405. The jounrney of life becomes very difficult if the eye-sight is lost.

406. One should never urinate in any water.

407. One should never dive into water fully naked.

408. One has knowledge like one's appearance.

409. One has wealth like one's knowledge.

410. Don't use fire to fight fire. Don't become angry with someone who is angry with you.

411. Those who practice austerities are honoured by all.

412. One should never think about having a relationship with a lady who belongs to someone else.

413. If one donates food that can wash sins one has commited.

414. Vedas provide excellent framework for righteousness.

415. A man should do some righteousness some how.

416. Truthfulness grants one the status of uninterrupted bliss.

417. No austerity in the world is greater than truthfulness.

418. Truthfulness is the means and Truthfulness is the end.

419. The harmony among people rests on truthfulness.

420. Many celestial favours are showered on the one who abides by truthfulness.

421. There is no sin greater than a false action.

422. We should not try to identify the defects in what our teachers say.

423. One should shun evil in all forms.

424. None is friendly to a cunning man.

425. A poor is always concerned about his life.

426. A person who shows bravery in giving charities is really brave.

427. Devotion to teachers and brahmanas is the embellishment of man.

Humility is the embellishment of a man.

429. A person who takes pride in his being a member of a great family and devoid of any great values is definitely inferior to a truthful person born in a low class family.

430. Good conduct causes rise in lifespan and glory.

431. One should not speak pleasing words to someone which will actually harm him.

432. Don't follow someone against the good of majority of people.

433. A person should not do any work in association with people who are base, cruel and bad.

434. Don't associate yourself with base people even though they have good fortune.

435. Always ensure that you reduce a loan, an enemy and a disease to zero.

436. He who has wealth leads a long and healthy life.

437. Don't offend someone who seeks something from you.

438. A base person will ask you to do something tough. He will offend you irrespective of whether the work fails, partially or fully succeeds.

439. A person who doesn't show any gratitude for the favours received can't save himself from the torments of hell.

440. A person's growth and doom depends on the sweet words and harsh words he speaks.

441. One may make his tongue of poison or nectar whatever he likes.

442. He who always do good to others don't have any enemies.

443. If you say something to Gods in praise they get pleased. Do you think that you can't please human-beings by speaking sweet words.

444. A word spoken with an intention of causing agony to others makes it's

marks on the mind of the listener for a long time.

445. One should not say unpleasing words to King or his representative.

446. A cuckoo pleases a human-being. One should speak sweet words based on truth to the King and keep him in good humour.

447. An effort for a bad action creates agony.

448. There is no place of honour in the society either to the one who seeks favour or to the one who is a wealthy miser.

449. A woman is embellished by the great fortune she creates by her commitment and loyalty to her family.

450. One should not destroy means of livelihood even of an enemy.

451. The land where water is easily available is better for agriculture.

452. One should not cause anger to a giant elephant by using petty castor.

453. A bondage of an elephant should be compatible with it's strength.

454. A kanher can't be used as a beater irrespective of it's length and thickness.

455. A firefly can't be used for creating fire whatever may be it's shine.

456. If someone flourishes in some areas that doesn't mean that he has virtue or dedication.

Section-5

457. A very old bark of a neem tree can't be used for making a knife. An evil remains useless irrespective of how old he grows.

458. One reaps what he sows.

459. One's intellect is conditioned by one's learning.

460. One's conduct is the reflection of one's family.

461. A neem tree won't become a mango tree irrespective of applying jaggery all over. Whatever discourse etc a bad person recieves he sticks to his meanness.

462. A certain little is better than an uncertain plenty.

463. One himself is the cause of one's misery and not others.

464. One should not travel in dark.

465. One should not go to sleep past mid-night.

466. When should one sleep, get up, eat, start journey all these things should be learnt from elders in the family or the intelligent people having experience.

467. One should not enter someone's house without necessary approval or reason.

468. People understand well by their intellect that they are not doing a good work. Still they don't desist from doing wrong.

469. Whatever customs people follow have been developed on the basis of scriptures.

470. One should follow what good people do if one is not able to understand scriptures.

471. A scripture is not more significant than good conduct.

472. A King knows far away developments as if he is watching everything with his eyes on the basis of information received from his spies.

473. Common people have herd mentality.

474. One should never despise one's means of livelihood.

475. The ultimate fruit of austerities is sense restraint.

476. It needs a high level of will power and austerities when one is enticed by sexual pleasures.

477. Sexual passions leads to evil outcomes.

478 – 479. One should not approach sex for deriving pleasures but for discharging one's responsibilities.

480. Those who work for social good should rise above sensual pleasures.

481. He is the knower of Vedas who knows the outcome of his austerities.

482. There is no permanent place for anyone in heaven. One enjoys stay in heaven as long as one's stock of merit is not exhausted.

483. There is no grief for a common man greater than losing physical comforts and happiness.

484. A person has so much attachment with his body that he won't agree to lose that even if he is offered status of Indra.

485. Salvation is the only remedy for all unhappiness.

486. A noble person as an enemy is better than an ignoble person as a friend.

487. Our family loses glory if we speak bad words.

488. In all worldly happiness birth of son is the highest.

489. Don't forget righteousness when you are in conflicts. One should abide by righteousness when conflicts arise.

490. One should plan all day's work after rising early in the morning.

491 He whose doom is not far away doesn't abide by good conduct.

492. One who is in need of milk should not keep an elephant.

493. If you want to win over people do charity to them.

494. One should not be impatient one wants to get something from others.

495. If you earn something by foul means that can't be used for something good.

496. Only a crow can eat a bitter fruit.

497. One should not think that a huge wealth will be of great use.

498. Whether water of a great ocean cannot be used for drinking purpose.

499. As a grain of sand maintains its hardness and distinct identity a vile person maintains his ego and doesn't mix with people.

500. Good people don't mix much with vile people.

501. A swan is never comfortable in a crematorium. Similarly good people don't like company of vile.

502. The whole world is engaged in action to make money.

503. Those who don't have discretion think that their desires should be fulfilled anyhow. They don't care about their duties and lose patience.

504. Those who are ruled by desires are devoid of wealth.

505. Those ruled by desires don't have patience backed by stability of mind.

506. It is better to die than to live a deprived life.

507. Desires destroy all diffidence and probity. Desires stoke the fire of greed.

508 One should not praise oneself.

509. One should not sleep during the day.

510. Those who are intoxicated by wealth don't listen to good advice from competent well- wishers.

511. A good woman regards her husband as most pious and sacred.

512. If a woman supports her husband in righteousness that leads to happiness and prosperity of the whole family.

513. One should respect guests coming all of a sudden and guests coming with a prior notice.

514. A charity done to an eligible donee never goes in vain.

515. If there arises any defect in the intelligence one considers one's enemy as one's friend.

516. A mirage is not water. Sensual pleasure is not happiness.

517. Those who don't have rigtheousness write fake books.

518. An association with a saintly person gives heavenly pleasure.

519. Good people behave the way they ask others to behave.

520. Appearance is the reflection of one's virtue.

521. One should reside at a place where there are comforts.

522. There is no deliverance for a treacherous person.

523. One should not get worried for the things happening in the course of destiny.

524 A good person considers problems faced by others as his own problems and takes efforts for solving their problems as he would have done for himself.

525. Those who are evil will hide their meanness and will only speak sweet words.

526. A foolish person deserves hatred.

527. One should not move without having necessary weapons to protect oneself.

528. One should never praise one's child.

529. Servants talk about the goodness of their master amidst people to make him popular.

530. Whenever dependent people do something good they attribute their work to their master.

531. One should not make unreasonable delay in executing the King's commands.

532. One should execute King's commands to the best of one's abilities.

533. Those who are intelligent don't have any enemies.

534. If you feel that some defect is about to set in your yourself you should not disclose it to others and try to rectify it.

535. One who demonstrates forgiveness performs his work successfully.

536. One should preserve some wealth for unforeseen contingencies.

537. One should join those who are walking the path of truth.

538. There is no need to postpone today's work tomorrow.

539. One should complete work to be done by noon in the morning itself.

540. The righteousness should be practical.

541. One who understands people on the basis of one's sharp intelligence should be considered as all knowing.

542. One who fails to understand people is a fool inspite of knowing scriptures.

543. The knowledge of sriptures should enable one understand things here and in the next world.

544. The power of discrimination that discerns good from bad illuminates the action.

545. Don't favour one at the cost of other.

546. Performance ranks higher than righteousness.

547. The soul is the witness of performance.

548. Soul is the witness for everything that happens.

549. One should not be a false witness.

550. Those who give false witness go to hell.

551. The five elements witness the sin that is commited in hiding.

552. A sinner glows his own sin.

553. A man's appearance speaks for the things going on in his mind.

554. It is impossible for anyone to prevent his face from speaking for his mind.

555. The rulers protect public money from thieves and people working for the rulers.

556. If the rulers create a bad image of themselves they lead to ruin of people.

557. The rulers who create a good image of themselves create happiness for their people.

558. People consider the rulers with equity like their mother.

559. A good ruler creates happiness in this world and gets heaven in the next world.

560. Non-violence is a mark of righteousness.

561. A good person takes same care of others that he takes of himself.

562. Animals are in every way unfit for human consumption. Men should never eat non-veg.

563. One who has the knowledge has no fear.

564. The lamp of knowledge puts an end to the fear of mundane existence.

565. The material happiness and all its contents are transient.

566. The body that is a place for germs, bacteria, stool and urine can work as a factor for earning merit or commiting sin.

567. The cycle of life and death is full of agony.

568. One can attain heaven on the basis of his austerities.

569. He who forgives furthers his austerities.

570. Austerities lead to accomplishment of all work.